HAITI
The First Black Republic
by Frantz Derenoncourt, Jr

Illustrated by, Eminence System

www.lfbookpublishing.com

Summary: A historical look into the fall and rise of Haiti,
which facilitated freedom from French and European rule.

ISBN 10: 0-9965411-4-4
ISBN 13: 978-0-9965411-4-5

Stay Connected with Frantz Derenoncourt, Jr. at www.frantzderenoncourt.com.

Dedicated

To Chase and Maven,
Make your ancestors proud!
Love, Daddy

Special Thanks:
Alicia Pearce Derenoncourt(wifey), Patricia Woolley(Auntie Fofo),
Marie Alice Woolley(Mom), Tupac Derenoncourt(Bro),
Frantz Derenoncourt, M.D.(Pops) and all my sisters,
brothers, cousins, aunts, uncles, and friends.
Thank you for your valuable input to make this
book what it has become. I'm forever grateful.

Very special thank you to my grandmothers
Mémere and Mommy Déde, and my grandfather
Daddy George. Thank you for all your sacrifices.

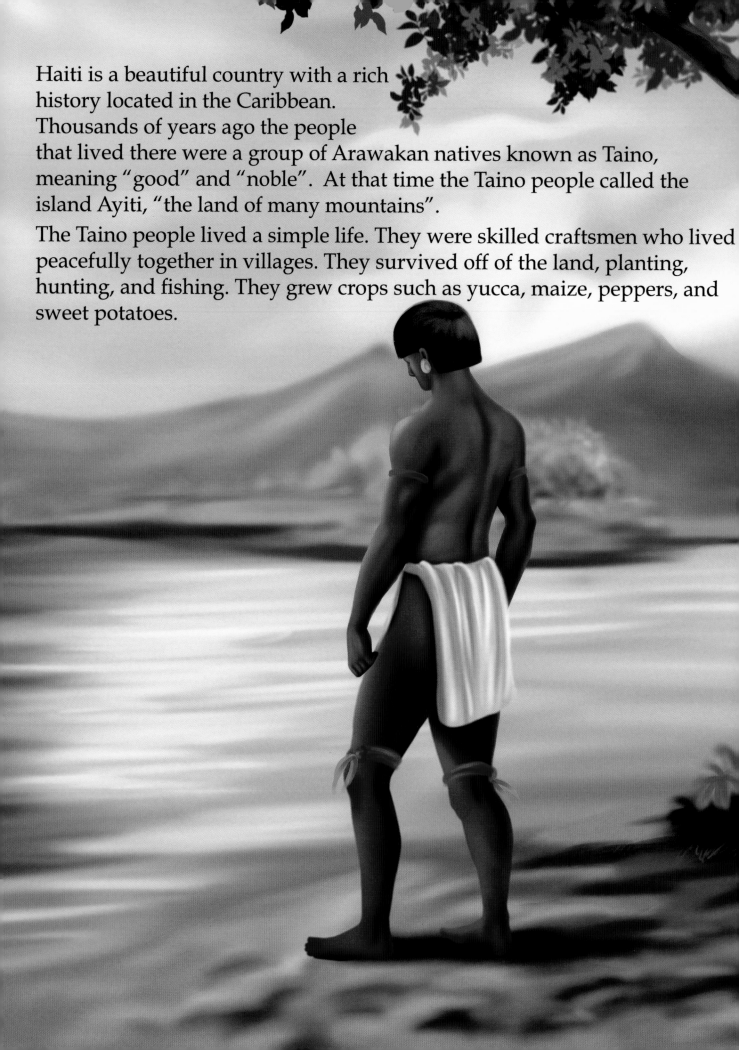

Haiti is a beautiful country with a rich history located in the Caribbean. Thousands of years ago the people that lived there were a group of Arawakan natives known as Taino, meaning "good" and "noble". At that time the Taino people called the island Ayiti, "the land of many mountains".

The Taino people lived a simple life. They were skilled craftsmen who lived peacefully together in villages. They survived off of the land, planting, hunting, and fishing. They grew crops such as yucca, maize, peppers, and sweet potatoes.

The Tainos enjoyed painting each other on their faces and bodies, singing folk songs, and performing dance ceremonies around fires for entertainment.
They loved nature and did not believe in possessions. They believed that everything belonged to Mother Earth and the people that needed it.

One day in December 1492, a large ship arrived on the beaches of Ayiti. On board the ship was a crew of men led by an explorer from the country of Spain named Christopher Columbus. His ship had been caught in the reef and become stranded. A group of Taino men eagerly rushed to Columbus to help haul the ship free. The friendly Tainos treated the Spaniards very kindly. Columbus had come to the island looking for gold.

The Taino led him and his men to parts of the island where gold was plentiful. Columbus loaded his ship with gold and other precious cargo to take back to Spain.

Though he did not really discover the island, Columbus planted the Spanish flag in the soil and claimed the island for Spain and renamed it Hispaniola.

Columbus left a group of Spanish people to build a fort called La Navida. The Spaniards took advantage of the Tainos and enslaved them. Most of the Tainos died from unfamiliar diseases brought back from Spain, as well as the labor they were forced to do. Between the years of 1492 and 1514, the population of Taino on the island fell from over one million people to less than twenty-five thousand.

The island of Hispaniola was very rich and all the gold, treasures, and everything it had to offer were taken to the kingdom of Spain. Other countries were noticing that Spain was thriving in their established colony of Hispaniola, where the land was fertile and natural resources grew abundantly

In the early 1600s, European newcomers began to inhabit the northwestern part of the island. The number of French began to grow rapidly and they even started building plantations and growing crops. The Spanish and French began competing for control of the island. In 1697, The Treaty of Ryswick was signed and the French and Spanish agreed to divide the island of Hispaniola in two. The Spanish side would be called Santo Domingo and the French side would be called Saint Domingue.

As tobacco, coffee, and sugar production started to increase in Saint Domingue, the French colonists were in growing need of a labor force to work on the plantations. They started bringing in people from Africa and making them slaves. The French slave masters forced the Africans to work on plantations all over the colony.

The French planters were very successful using this system and it made the slave masters very rich. At its peak, Saint Domingue provided two thirds of the world's sugar. Saint Domingue became one of the world's most flourishing and wealthiest colonies.

The French called Saint Domingue "The Pearl of The Antilles".

Even though the French planters were becoming wealthy from the land, the enslaved Africans were not happy. The work was very hard and many of the slave masters did not treat the slaves nicely. The slave masters did not pay the slaves for their work and gave them very little time to eat, drink, and rest. The slaves labored from sun up to sun down, cutting down sugar canes and harvesting the coffee and tobacco crops.

The slave masters would beat the slaves to make them work harder and intimidate the other workers. As a result, since most of the slaves did not survive the beatings and harsh treatment, the slave masters were always replenishing the amount of laborers by enslaving more Africans to keep the plantation system profitable.

Many of the slaves ran away from the plantations because they were being treated so badly by their slave masters. Most of them would hide in the mountains so they would not be found. The slaves that escaped to the mountains were called Maroons. One of the most famous Maroons was a man called Mackandal.

Mackandal fled towards the mountains and he persuaded a lot of the other slaves to join him. Soon, he convinced thousands of slaves to fight against the injustice of slavery.

Mackandal was not satisfied with the few thousand Maroons who escaped the bad treatment from the slave masters. He wanted freedom for all the slaves of Saint Domingue. Mackandal organized an army from the Maroons in the mountains and created a plan to defeat the slave masters and free all the slaves.

He led his army of Maroons at night and raided different plantations on the island, liberating thousands of slaves.

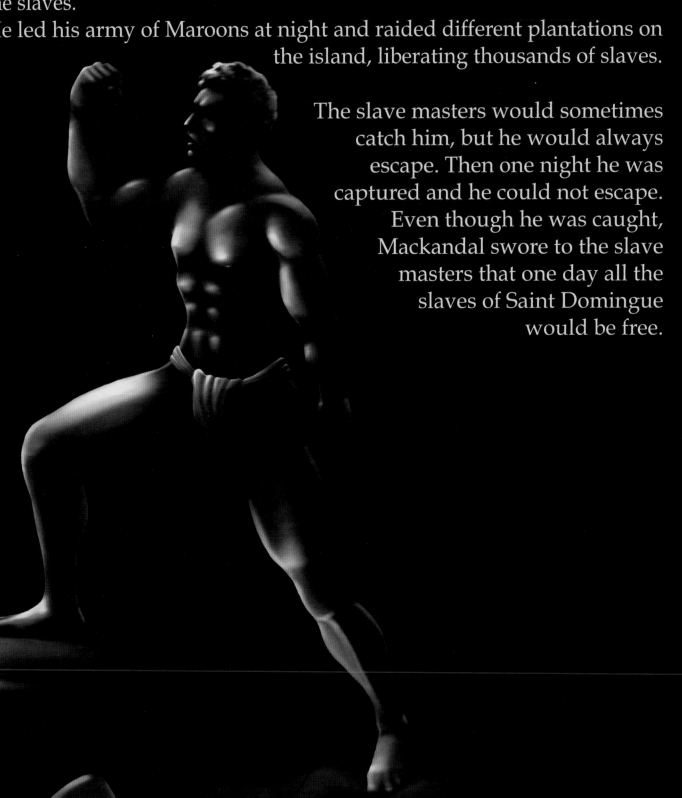

The slave masters would sometimes catch him, but he would always escape. Then one night he was captured and he could not escape. Even though he was caught, Mackandal swore to the slave masters that one day all the slaves of Saint Domingue would be free.

Thirty three years after Mackandal was captured, the slaves were still working and being mistreated on the plantations of Saint Domingue under the brutal whip of the French slave masters. It was around this time that a slave named Dutty Boukman, brought from the island of Jamaica, started what would become the biggest slave revolt in the history of the world.

Boukman was a spiritual man. On August 14, 1791, Boukman conducted a secret ceremony, along with the mambo Cecile Fatiman, in a thickly wooded area under the tree of Bois Caiman, in which he inspired the slaves to take action. They laid out detailed plans for defeating the French and setting all the slaves on the island free.

After the ceremony, slaves on plantations all over the north of
Saint Domingue began to rise up against their slave masters.
They burned the plantations to the ground and fought back against
their oppressors. The slaves would band together and go from plantation
to plantation, freeing other slaves and defeating their masters.
Even though Boukman did not survive the fighting, he became one
of the great heroes of what will go down in history as
The Haitian Revolution.

When the French government heard about the slave revolt in Saint Domingue, they sent 10,000 French soldiers to the island to crush the rebellion. Even though Boukman was killed, the revolt was still going on. But in order to truly defeat the French and bring freedom to the slaves, the rebels needed a new leader. The leader that would emerge was an ex-slave named Toussaint Louverture.

Toussaint joined the revolution as a doctor but quickly rose to the top of the ranks to lead the revolutionary army. Toussaint was a brilliant leader. He could read and write, which was something most of the slaves could not do. Toussaint organized and trained the rebel army on how to properly fight against the experienced French army. He was also a great speaker who motivated and inspired the rebels in times of despair.

Toussaint led the revolutionary army, along with his top officers, Jean-Jacques Dessalines and Henri Christophe. He led them to victory after victory over the French army. In 1794, the French suffered great losses and they had no other choice but to abolish slavery and free all the slaves of Saint Domingue.

Toussaint was made Governor General of the colony and protected the island from foreign powers such as Spain and England for many years to come. He became the most powerful man in Saint Domingue from 1794 to 1802. Toussaint's achievements during his years in power include social reforms, structuring and organizing a new government, establishing courts of justice, and building public schools.

In 1799, Napoleon Bonaparte came into power in France and two years later sent a force of 20,000 soldiers on 86 war ships to Saint Domingue led by his brother in law, General Charles Leclerc, to take over the colony and reinstitute slavery.

Toussaint was tricked into a meeting with Leclerc where he was captured and put on a boat to France. Toussaint warned his captors with this phrase: "In overthrowing me, you have done no more than cut down the trunk of the tree of the black liberty in Saint Domingue – it will spring back from the roots, for they are numerous and deep".

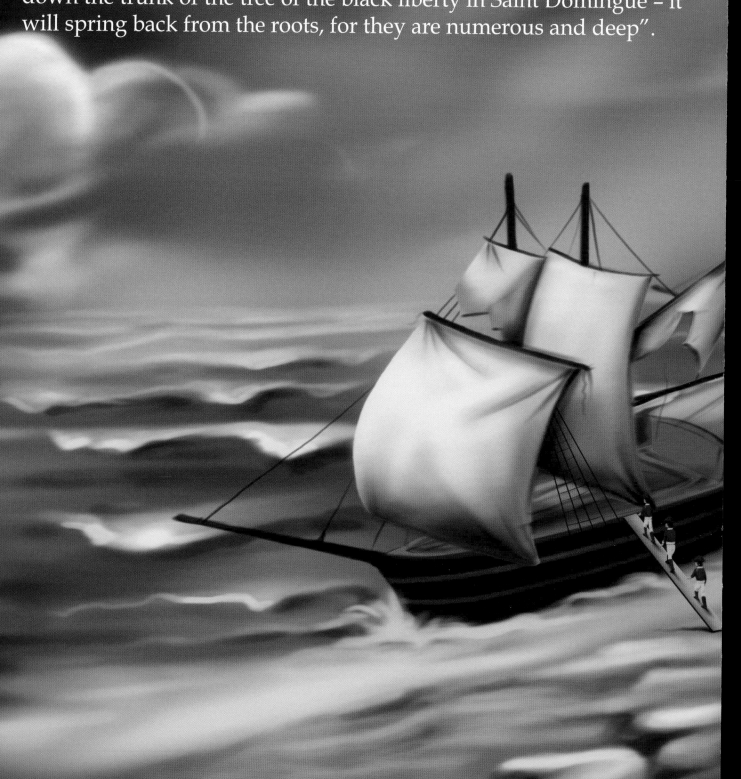

Napoleon locked Toussaint up in a prison high in the French Alps called Fort de Joux, where he would spend the remaining days of his life.

Toussaint Louverture passed away from malnutrition and pneumonia on April 7, 1803.

The fight for freedom had started again.

There were many fierce battles between the rebel army and Napoleon's army. General Leclerc and thousands of his soldiers were stricken with Yellow Fever and lost their lives. The rebel army used the fever as an opportunity to gain the upper hand in the war.

November 18, 1803 would be one of the most famous battles in this war of independence, the Battle of Vertieres. Leclerc's successor, General Rochambeau, desperately tried to hang onto one of the French army's few remaining strongholds, Fort Vertieres. However, General Dessalines along with General Francois Capois led the charge that would not only defeat the French once and for all, but to rid Saint Domingue of slavery forever.

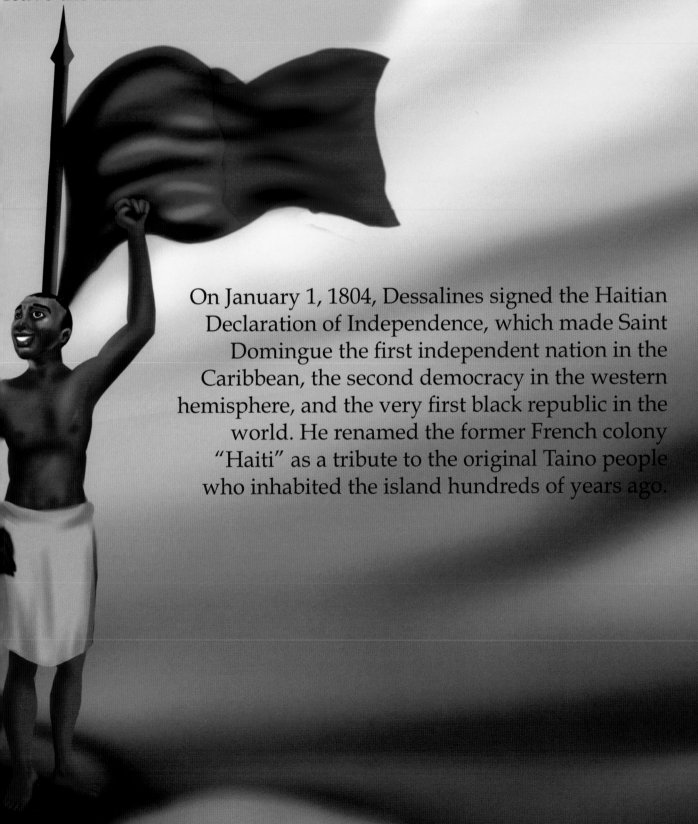

After winning the Battle of Vertieres, General Dessalines was successful in forcing the French army to completely surrender and leave the island.

On January 1, 1804, Dessalines signed the Haitian Declaration of Independence, which made Saint Domingue the first independent nation in the Caribbean, the second democracy in the western hemisphere, and the very first black republic in the world. He renamed the former French colony "Haiti" as a tribute to the original Taino people who inhabited the island hundreds of years ago.

Important Dates

- 1492   Columbus lands on Ayiti and renames it Hispaniola, little Spain
- 1697   The Treaty of Ryswick is signed and Spain cedes the western part of Hispaniola to France. The French names it's territory Saint Domingue
- 1750s   The Mackandal Rebellions
- 1791   Boukman's secret ceremony beginning the slave revolts
- 1794   France abolishes slavery in all their colonies
- 1796   Toussaint Louverture is appointed Commander in Chief of Saint Domingue and later becomes Governor General
- 1802   Napoleon sends the French army to invade Saint Domingue and reinstitute slavery
- 1802   Toussaint Louverture is captured and sent to a French prison
- 1803   The Battle of Vertieres, Generals Jean-Jacques Dessalines and Francois Capois are immortalized
- 1804   Jean-Jacques Dessalines declares an independent Haiti

Did You Know???

- In 1915, The United States invaded Haiti and occupied the country for 19 years. That occupation also met resistance by rebel leaders like Charlamagne Peralte.

- Frederick Douglass was the United States Ambassador to Haiti from 1889-1891.

- In 1825, Haiti was forced to pay an indemnity to France in the amount of 160,000,000 francs(comparable to $40 billion in 2010 currency) for loss of property (the slaves). It would take Haiti over 100 years to pay. Even though it was paid in full, the affect of the debt has crippled Haiti's economy to this day.

- In 1805, the King of North Haiti, Henri Christophe began construction of the Citadelle to keep Haiti safe from European invaders. The massive fort required 20,000 workers and over 15 years to complete. To this day the Citadelle is the largest fortress in the Western Hemisphere and one of Haiti's top tourist attractions.

- After Haiti defeated France in the revolutionary war, Napoleon gave up on his plans for Western domination, leading to the Louisiana Purchase, which doubled the size of the United States.

- The leaders of the three largest slave revolts in the United States, Gabriel Prosser (1800), Nat Turner (1822) and Denmark Vesey (1831), were inspired by the success of the Haitian Revolution.

Bio

Frantz Derenoncourt, Jr. is a first generation Haitian-American born and raised in East Flatbush, Brooklyn, NY. After very humble beginnings he attended Virginia State University in Petersburg, VA where he majored in Business Management and soon after moved to the nations capitol, Washington, DC. After working a few 9 to 5 jobs around town, Frantz fell in love with the real estate industry and found success as a real estate sales associate and real estate investor.

As a child growing up in Brooklyn in the early 80s, Frantz was often picked on for being Haitian. Teachers could never pronounce his name correctly and the students would always have a cruel Haitian joke on hand. At times, he felt ashamed to be Haitian until he started reading about Haitian history. The fact that his little country accomplished something that no other nation had accomplished at that time gave him a tremendous sense of pride. He started reading everything he could get his hands on in regards to the Haitian Revolution and relaying the stories to his son, Chase. When he saw that his son was just as excited as he was, Frantz then realized that this fascinating story needs to be told in a way that even a 2nd grade reader can appreciate the accomplishment of his ancestors. Thus, Haiti: The First Black Republic was born.

Mission Statement

My mission for this book is to establish a sense of pride in the black youth all over the world. I also aim to tell the stories of success and victory when we come together as a people against impossible odds.

I also write to let the world know that if you're a person of color from Haiti, Dominican Republic, Cuba, the United States or any other nation, all of our ancestors came from the same place. A win for one of us, is a win for all of us.